HIP EXPECTATIC

How to get through a hip replacement by someone who should know better

MR JONATHAN HULL MD FRCS (ORTH) CONSULTANT
ORTHOPAEDIC SURGEON
(The Patient)

Magic Daisy Publishing

First published 2022 by Magic Daisy Publishing
Printed through Amazon

www.magicdaisypublishing.co.uk

ISBN 979-8-4040-0426-7

Printed and bound by Amazon

Jonathan was educated at Uppingham School and Birmingham University Medical School, graduating in 1983. He joined the Army and served for 19 years with postings to Germany and the USA and operational tours in Northern Ireland, Iraq, Congo, Bosnia and Kosovo. He was parachute trained and provided surgical support for UK Special Forces.

After leaving the Army he was a Consultant Orthopaedic Surgeon at Frimley Park Hospital from 1999-2020, specialising in all aspects of hip surgery as well as trauma management.

Jonathan is married and has four grown-up children and two grandchildren. He has now retired from NHS practice and lives in Norfolk where, as it happens, he grew up. He shoots regularly at Bisley and has represented Hampshire, England and Great Britain.

He injured his right hip parachuting in 1996. Eventually he reluctantly accepted it needed sorting out and he underwent a hip replacement in November 2021.

FOREWORD

When it became apparent that I would need a new hip, Richard, my surgeon, knowing that he had two consultant colleagues to do, decided that buddying us up and putting himself through the stress of both on the same list was the best idea! Who knows how he coped with the stress of that, as having operated on colleagues I am only too aware of the sleepless nights it engenders. Perhaps he was of the 'in for a penny…in for a pound' opinion and felt he might as well worry about us at the same time as on two separate lists. Whatever the motivation, from a patient's point of view the decision was inspired. I got to spend two nights in hospital with Jonathan who was already a senior consultant when I was appointed, and who looked after me, and dare I say it made my stay in hospital amusing and even a pleasure, though the fact that it was my first 'holiday' out of the home for 18 months due to the pandemic, may have made it seem a touch more exciting than it was! Remarkably our senses of humour were very well aligned. Being surgical however, the vast majority of our ruminations are entirely unrepeatable, but we will both blame the drugs for at least some of that!

They say that a little knowledge is a dangerous thing… In my case that little knowledge was two stints as a junior surgeon nearly 25 years ago. I was woefully out of date which was probably worse than having no knowledge at all. Not everyone can have a Jonathan sitting across the corridor, or on the end of a phone line or messaging service, before, during and after an inpatient stay to encourage and cajole, but this honest and open book is the next best thing. It encompasses all of the things that caused me to reach for Google at 4am when the hip pain had woken me in my pre-op weeks and months, and the little things I worried about post-op.

Importantly, the information I craved was the sort of practical, down-to-earth, advice that this book contains, and it is as relevant to a Professor of Orthopaedic Surgery as to the non-medical patient. I wish it had been available before my operation and am sure it will benefit a great many people in the future. Thanks for everything Jonathan!

Mr Henry Tilney MD FRCS
Consultant Colorectal Surgeon
December 2021

INDEX

PREFACE

THE CHANCES ARE YOU KNEW WHAT THEY WERE GOING TO SAY. After all the months of waiting for an appointment and your GP telling you that the hip x-ray showed 'a little wear and tear', you probably weren't surprised to find you needed a hip replacement.

Up to that point, the idea of an operation was something slightly vague and what other people had. You know plenty of people who have had new hips and celebrities always let the world know when they have one. That's all fine in the abstract, but, it's a *completely different matter* when you take in that this time, it's you we're talking about. The remainder of the consultation passes in a blur. The surgeon is trying to tell you all about hip replacements, what the implants are made of, how long they last etc, and all you can think about is the fact that sometime soon, someone is going to cut you open from hip to knee, rip out your old joint and hammer in a new one. There's going to be blood; there's going to be bone; there's definitely going to be pain. Somewhere in the distance you can hear him or her saying you will only need to be in hospital for two or three nights (yeah right!) and can expect to be off your crutches in a few weeks, but to be honest about 5% of what you get told at that appointment actually goes in. You feel like a rabbit in the headlights - but so does everyone else so don't worry.

I have just been through the whole process and have now had my new hip. I am supposed to know what I am talking about so I will try and make some sense of it for those of you who don't happen to be hip surgeons.

By the way, that thing about it being different when it's you?

I had that too.

IN THE BEGINNING

Most people, the vast majority, develop hip arthritis slowly over several years and there is no specific point where they remember that their hip becomes painful and stiff. A very few, like me, had some sort of injury that started things off but even then, it is usually months or years before things become bad enough to worry about.

If you fracture your hip joint in an accident, say, then from that point onwards, despite whatever brilliant surgery you had to fix the break, it's quite likely that one day the hip will give in and fail. Joints, especially the surface cartilage layers, are quite vulnerable and slowly change from being perfectly smooth to looking like crazy-paving, and this is what causes the inflammation and pain. People gradually become aware that the hip is sore, is getting stiffer, that socks are becoming harder to get on and that the hip aches after exercise or even a long walk.

Where is hip pain usually felt? The actual ball and socket joint is quite near the front of the body, in the middle of the groin on each side, so that's the main place, often causing what is initially thought to be a 'groin strain'. It is commonly described as a deep 'toothache' type of discomfort and people grip their sides pushing their fingers into the groin to try and ease it off. It is what I would call a *nasty* pain, and not one you can rub better. It's deep and it's 'worrying' - you just know it's not going to go on its own.

Sometimes the pain is more on the side, over what people think of as the hip proper, and lying on that side at night can be painful. There are even some people who only get referred pain down to the thigh and the knee, and the hip doesn't seem to hurt at all. These can be tricky to work out and sometimes even we surgeons may be unsure if the hip is really the source of the discomfort. Also the lower back may cause referred pain around the side of the hip and mimic true hip symptoms. So, if the pain can be misleading, what else can be causing trouble? It's unusual for a significantly diseased hip joint not to cause some degree of stiffness and restriction of movement. Again this may not be dramatic at first and you gradually come to recognise that your leg doesn't move as freely as it used to.

Bending over, putting on socks and shoes, cutting toenails etc, can all get just a little more difficult, again gradually, and without some sudden change. Of course, we are very good at adapting, so you can quite easily become fairly stiff in the hips without really knowing it. If you have a supple back and no knee problems, then it is perfectly possible to think that the hip movement is absolutely fine - all you are doing is using the flexibility of other joints to get round the problem. It's good that we can do that, but it may slow down the time to diagnosis.

Generally, sitting and lying is not a problem; it is getting about that starts to be limited. Runners find they can't go as far without pain, walkers start needing walking poles and sportsmen find increasingly frequent reasons why they can't go to training that week.

Hip pain can be quite wearing and people get tired without knowing why and put things off. The lawn doesn't get mowed that week, you take the car to the shops instead of walking and, for some couples, even having sex can become uncomfortable enough to put them off.

The other symptom that people sometimes get and don't understand is clicking or clunking from the hip. This is not so common but can be quite alarming whether or not it is associated with pain. Sometimes it's the actual joint which is the wrong shape or has irregular surfaces and sometimes it's the tendons around the joint snapping over it.

So how do these symptoms affect you overall? Limping is common and the patient is sometimes the last to know. I used to be regularly told I was limping but hadn't realised it. In clinic I always ask partners if the patient limps and they are often more reliable than the one with the hip problem.

Cars are not good for bad hips. Getting in and out can become really quite awkward and most people find the 'mermaid' works well – you sit down first, lock the knees together and swing both legs in and out. This is easier with a bigger car, of course. Oh, and always park with a decent gap on the driver's side (and hope no-one sneaks in close while you're away).

One of the main things that drives patients towards treatment is disturbed sleep. Most people lie on their sides to sleep and if a hip is sore, it tends to wake you up. Eventually you give up and end up dozing in a chair because that stops you rolling onto your side. So many patients, me included, have finally decided to get treatment because of sleep disturbance.

NOW WHAT?

So, if hip arthritis is gradual and insidious and there's no clear point when something needs to be done, at what stage do you see someone about it? A common pattern is for your GP to arrange some physiotherapy for you and prescribe painkillers and/or anti-inflammatories. This seems to help at first - and then it doesn't. Eventually your physio may ask the GP to take things further. Maybe an x-ray gets done at this point and it shows that there is indeed something going wrong in the hip.

Or maybe not… Surprise surprise, your x-ray doesn't show very much. The report the GP gets back says there are 'minimal changes'. This is hard to hear because you *know* it hurts and surely there should be something to show for it?

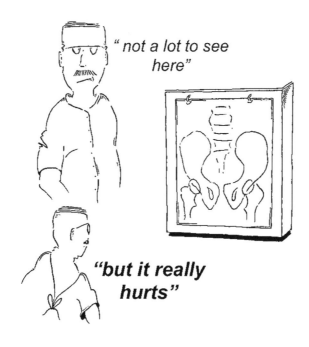

Unfortunately, it does take quite a long time for the x-rays to change after the hip becomes inflamed, sometimes more than a year, so your symptoms may seem to be much worse than your x-ray suggests they should be. There's not a lot we can do about that except continue to try and treat your symptoms as well as we can.

There will come a point where it's all getting too difficult to live with and hopefully your doctor will then refer you onto the hospital to be seen by an orthopaedic surgeon. Just at the moment, this process has been quite disrupted by the pandemic and there may be a long wait for people to be seen and then once seen, to get in for surgery. Some people use their savings to bypass the system and get things done on the private side, but for those who can't it can be a difficult time as the process has slowed right down.

Assuming the best, you get an appointment and you're off to see the consultant. This is the point where in my preface I mentioned that the idea of having a hip replacement probably isn't that worrying as lots of other people have had them and you know that they work. The moment the consultant says *you* need one though, that all changes. Suddenly it's all about you and you realise that this is ONE BIG DEAL.

Most of the rest of the conversation goes in one ear and out the other, and it is well-recognised that patients tend to be like 'rabbits in the headlights' once they have been given a diagnosis and remember little of what was said after that. Don't worry, there should be plenty of information out there on the Internet and, with information sheets to supplement what you've already been told, it should be easy enough to get the information you require. One of the reasons for writing this book is to try and make this easier in a way that people can appreciate, as I have only just finished going through the process.

Once the decision is made then of course there's the question of when. At present it's unlikely that any dates will be offered and you will simply find yourself on a waiting list which may take months or even years to come round. If you have the means to go ahead privately, then it's probable that dates will be discussed and finally you can start working towards a definitive solution to the problem.

Do not be surprised if suddenly your pain gets worse. It's quite common that once the diagnosis is made and you've actually seen what's going on on the x-rays, it will also seem much more uncomfortable than it was. You now have a good reason to feel pain which tends to make it feel worse. You now have a defining label: you are arthritic! That may not worry you too much if you're 85, but if you're 40 it can be quite shattering to think that you've already worn out your joint to the point where it needs replacing. Many patients have had a new hip before the age of 50 but it is quite shocking to actually be one of that group.

Time is very likely to drag out. You know what needs doing but there's a big gap between the decision point and the actual event. In many ways your life will feel as if it's on hold because you can't make plans (holidays, job changes etc) until it's all been sorted. Information may be difficult to get and finding when your operation date is likely to be hard. The system at least guarantees that eventually you will get your operation and hopefully people will be done in the right priority order so that you know that at least if you're waiting, other people worse than you are getting their interventions more promptly.

That may not be much consolation but it's the best I can offer.

IT'S GETTING SERIOUS NOW

Planning for admission

YOU HAVE A DATE!!!

After months of patiently waiting, your consultant's secretary has called and you have agreed a date for your operation. Or to be strictly accurate, you have just agreed to whatever date is offered. Never mind that you were meant to be going on holiday then or your daughter is due to have her first baby on that very day, or that it's due to be your first day in that dream job you have waited for forever. Unless you have a life-threatening reason to decline this offered date, you will take it.

Actually, most secretaries will be happy to work around dates and you have much more opportunity to request one that suits you than you realise. I can tell you not to worry about trying to negotiate, but the chances are you're not going to risk it.

Dates can change for all sorts of reasons. Hospital beds are not always available. Staff (even surgeons) can get ill, or at least test positive for Covid-19. Trains can derail and planes can crash, but it's actually not at all common for elective surgery dates to be changed at short notice. Everyone knows someone who had it changed ten times before they got in. Of course they do, and they make sure you do too.

Have faith, the risk is low and it won't be you.
Promise? Er...

Anyway, there it is, your special date in the diary. There is lots to think about now.

Time off

How much time off will you need? This depends on what you do for a living. If you work outside and need to be physically active, then three months. If you work from home and can sit to do it, something many have continued doing after the lockdowns, then how about one week?

Common sense applies more than rigid rules. Clearly if you commit to being available one week post op and have anything other than a perfect hospital experience, this may be far too soon. It is very common for hip replacement patients to feel thoroughly washed out for several weeks after getting home. It's a big operation and most patients lose more than a cupful of blood. Almost everyone is a bit anaemic for a few weeks and this has a very wearying effect making everything just, well, harder to do.

Have a really good think and err on the safe side. I would not recommend actually *going* to work, whatever you do, for a month at least. If you progress well in the first few weeks, then great, crack on. If it's not so fast and it's taking longer to get mobile, make provision to extend that to two months. Employers are generally flexible and will not want you back if you're a liability or you go all droopy at your desk. The worst at this are the self-employed and they usually need some firm advice to TAKE IT EASY.

Case study: me. I'm a hip surgeon (yes, ironic I know). I am taking 8 weeks off and have booked operations to do in week 9. I have also warned these patients that if I fail to recover to a safe standard of function, their operations will have to be postponed. But, I *will* be doing telephone clinics after 10 days which is perfectly reasonable and safe and the only risk to my patients is that I might be a bit wriggly on the line. If I still need strong pain medication by then, I will defer the appointments, as I wouldn't want to be working when effectively a bit tiddly.

Driving

This is the most important milestone for lots of people and it iis bound up with the return to work time for many as well.

Simple rules:

Rule 1. Safety. You absolutely *must* be able to drive safely. In effect this means that you can do an emergency stop, every time. If it's your right hip, then suddenly jamming on the brakes may be restricted by weakness and pain. If you're slow, and you crash, you may never forgive yourself or have any money. If it's the left side it's not so much of a problem, and if it's an automatic, well then only rule 2 applies.

Rule 2. Comfort. Getting into, sitting in, and getting out of a car should be simple and not painful. Some car seats aren't great for people with a hip wound and the wrap-around bucket seats, although lovely normally, can be a real pain. Cushions, rubber rings, etc may have a place. Don't forget, there may be traffic and this may grind to a halt at times. Imagine being in the middle lane of the M25 going nowhere and your hip is really painful. For three hours. Get the point?

Patients always ask us when they can drive. The rules just say that the driver must be in full control of the car at all times. Insurance companies often ask patients to get 'permission' to drive from their doctor. Unless I missed it, we were not given training on how to assess driving ability and we certainly don't go and sit in the patient's car to see how they are doing. We are not qualified to make that call. But you are. Common sense again.

When you are ready, give it a go somewhere quiet, with a witness. You need an objective view on whether you're safe and can do emergency stops, and if disaster does ever strike, that can be invaluable in court. Look at it this way, if you sprained your right ankle you wouldn't drive until you felt safe to do so would you? It's the same principle after a hip replacement.

My guidance: Right hip: 6 weeks. Left hip: 3 weeks. 'ish.

Pre-op assessment

THIS IS IMPORTANT SO PAY ATTENTION.

In the (good?) old days, patients were admitted for surgery and some tests were done at that point. Usually the results were back before the operation began but not so much if you were first on the list. Sometimes, those test results meant that it would not be safe to proceed with surgery on that day so the patient was regretfully expelled from the hospital, although usually after a cup of NHS tea and a biscuit.

As a surgeon that meant an early bath, plus much frustration that valuable operating time had been wasted. More recently, it has been found to be very cost effective for those same tests to be done a few weeks in advance of the operation so that, if there has to be a delay for patient A, lucky patient B can be fitted in their place. There is also a chance that patient A may have the problem rectified in time for the original date.

These tests are chosen to make sure that common reasons for the patient not being fit for surgery are picked up. These are things like anaemia, silent kidney failure, heart irregularities etc. They are not common and the majority of patients sail through, but for the few, it is much better to be delayed and sorted out, than to either be turned away on the day, or worse, put at risk by going ahead in ignorance (that first patient on the list thing mentioned earlier).

Pre-op assessment is done by experienced nurses who have access to clever anaesthetists if oddities are picked up. They have a lot of responsibility and take their role extremely seriously.

I had never given much thought to pre-op until it was my turn and it rather dawned on me that this could be a show-stopper for all my carefully laid plans. What if something is picked up and I can't have my operation? All the time off afterwards, the operations after 8 weeks etc, would have to be changed. More to the point my hip was really sore by then and I wanted it to be gone. Fortunately, like most people, I passed all the tests and there was no phone call with bad news. It is quite nice to know I don't appear to have any lurking side issues for the immediate future. It's like getting an MOT with no failures. It doesn't mean you won't ever break down but it stops you worrying about it for a while.

Covid concerns

Hopefully this part will be consigned to history before long but I'll include it for completeness - and in case there are new variants waiting to emerge. All elective operating stopped in April 2020. Everyone was put on hold and, by the time we started up again in the summer, some changes had been put in place. It was clear that hospitals were good breeding grounds for the virus and that inpatients were getting it. Some of those were dying.

For elective surgery, that had to be avoided at all costs and therefore all patients needed to have a negative PCR test three days in advance of their admission, and then they had to self-isolate until they came in. For higher risk cases, that isolation period was 14 days. It was assumed, rightly so, that if all staff were tested regularly, there should be very little risk of catching Covid in hospital as long as elective patients were walled off from everyone else. This is the basis of the so-called Green Pathway, and it works.

More recently, for double jabbed patients, the isolation requirement has gone and two Lateral Flow Tests (LFTs) are sufficient, one 48 hours before and one immediately before admission. For those of us who have been doing LFTs and uploading the results for months, this is not a problem of course. For the elderly patient who has not, maybe it's different. Hopefully the tech that most of us find easy and 'normal for now' is not too stressful for some patients who, as I am well aware, are already somewhat tense.

What else?

Post-discharge, which is usually on day 3, the patient cannot be on their own. By that I mean, there *must* be someone at home most of the time. I'll go as far to say that I refuse to operate until there is a plan for this in place. The reason is simple: in order to achieve a decent outcome, two crutches must be used for at least four weeks. It is vital that the muscles around the hip heal properly and, if they do not, there will always be a limp and probably pain.

With the best will in the world, you simply cannot look after yourself using two crutches at all times. Trays are impossible to carry. Anti-embolism stockings are impossible to get on without help, and the risk of falling is dramatically worse if there is no-one to call for help.

I KNOW THIS BECAUSE I HAVE BEEN TESTING THIS THEORY SINCE I GOT HOME.

I am young (ish) and strong. My arms have benefitted from daily press-ups for three months before my operation. I have good balance and am well-coordinated. And I *could not* manage on my own - so that proves it. You must have someone, or if that is not possible, a convalescent home or equivalent should be booked for at least three weeks after discharge.

At the absolute least, district nurse visits three times per day and a very well-stocked freezer with ready-meals might do, but the risk goes up as soon as you are alone in an empty house.

Hip replacement is a really effective and safe intervention with massive benefits. It is NOT ACCEPTABLE to risk even a fair outcome by making poor, or no, discharge arrangements.

DO. NOT. TRY. AND. MANAGE. ON. YOUR. OWN.

Pre-op exercises

Physiotherapists will certainly advise these and I am sure they are a good idea. Optimising core strength, maintaining hip mobility and trying to avoid tightness at the front of the hip by periods of lying on your front are all beneficial. Your physio will be able to advise exactly what you should do. In addition, improving your arm strength is a really good idea, both for using crutches and also when it comes to lowering yourself onto the loo (see the Addendum on page 46).

Confession: Apart from doing daily press-ups, I didn't do many actual hip exercises. I wish I had, as my hip flexor was really painful post-op, which I will describe in detail later.

THE TECHNICAL BIT

Before I describe my hospital experience, I need to cover the more technical features of hip replacement, the sort of information you will have been given in advance, and the important aspects of the operation. I will also explain the potential risks.

Hip replacement is an extremely successful intervention, alleviating the symptoms of 90-95% of patients within 6 months.

Never lose sight of that. It's why we do it; it works.

Since the 1950's, the operation has developed gradually, with various changes of method and materials and it continues to be improved with newer technologies and techniques. We will probably look back in 30 years time and wonder why they did it that way in 2021, as I suspect by then we will have biological joint replacements - your own tissue, grown in a lab and implanted back, for ever. But that's the future.

As for the now, the operation is pretty standard. The hip joint is exposed, the diseased ball and socket are removed, and new metal and ceramic or polyethylene prostheses are implanted. The vast majority of hip implants have been used for some years now and data on their performance has been available through the National Joint Registry since 2003. The pioneering days of the late 20th century, when it would seem that surgeons were trying out new materials more or less on a whim, have ended. It is now impossible to use something new without rigorous oversight, controlled trials and extended monitoring. This is a good thing as we have something that works so well as it is, but as long as it is properly regulated, we should never try to prevent innovation.

Implants: Wherever you go in UK, you will get a standard implant via a standard approach.

In a nutshell, your hip will either be cemented in or rely on a press-fit (uncemented), and the metal components will be either titanium, cobalt chrome alloy, or stainless steel. The bearing surface, where the head meets the socket, will either be ceramic-on-ceramic, ceramic-on-plastic or metal-on-plastic. Simple.

Sort of. Cemented implants are a better option for the older patient whose bone may not be robust enough to cope with an uncemented hip. There is pressure to use cement in all patients over 70, and certainly this is more or less mandatory for the over 80's. This is not the place to discuss their relative merits but your surgeon will be able to do so if you ask.

Patients often ask me how much a hip replacement weighs. I think some assume that it must be quite heavy, but in fact the total weight of the implants is only slightly more than the weight of the the bone that has been removed. If you were hoping for a reason for that post-op weight gain, sorry.

Approach: The hip joint can be safely accessed from the front, the side or the back.

The front approach is newer, technically more difficult, and has less history but avoids cutting so much muscle. We probably need a few more years to really evaluate this, but the results are very promising.

The side approach is more popular in the north of UK and may be technically simpler for the surgeon in training. More muscle is incised and repaired, making careful rehab essential while it heals.

The posterior approach is more common in the south and avoids as much muscle dissection as the side version, but the dislocation rate may be slightly higher, although this complication is now very rare.

Each surgeon will have his or her way of doing the operation and will be as perfected in that technique as they can be. It makes no sense to demand either a particular approach or type of implant if that is not your surgeon's usual practice.

Anaesthesia: Your anaesthetist is most likely to suggest you have a spinal anaesthetic with, or occasionally without, sedation. Local anaesthetic is injected into the spine, numbing and paralysing everything below the waist within 10 minutes. It lasts 4-6 hours, plenty long enough for the operation and the first part of recovery. It is low risk, good for the circulation and helps prevent deep vein thrombosis (DVT) – more on DVT later. The sedation is a very light general anaesthetic, just enough to keep you asleep and, without the spinal in place, it would not stop you feeling even the very first incision. It wears off rapidly (minutes) leaving no grogginess.

The alternative is a full general anaesthetic (GA). Some patients will need this for good clinical reasons (eg. a fused spine which will not allow the needle to get into the right place), but more commonly it is used because the patient cannot bear the idea of having a spinal. When explained properly and gently, spinals are usually agreed to by the patient in the end. The disadvantages of GA are sometimes prolonged grogginess afterwards, and the hip is painful from the moment you are awake in recovery, making pain control more difficult to manage than when a spinal slowly wears off giving time to get the pain medicine working.

Tip: Have the spinal. No question.

POTENTIAL COMPLICATION

It is so important that patients go into surgery with an understanding of the potential important complications. Informed consent is key, and no-one should agree to be operated on without having heard and appreciated what could possibly go wrong. The days of blindly following doctors' orders on the assumption that 'we know best' are long gone and, although not everyone wants to know all of the downsides to surgery, there are some things that are non-negotiable and you must hear them.

Hip replacement is safe. This means that the vast majority get through it without anything going wrong at all and end up with a brilliant outcome. NEVER LOSE SIGHT OF THAT.

However, the things that may spoil a good outcome are as follows:

Infection: Bacterial infection in a hip replacement can be very difficult to cure without removing the implants. Although unlikely to be life-threatening, infection can lead to progressive loosening of the prostheses which then move against the bone causing increasing pain and disability. Although it can happen: I don't mean severe sepsis here with abscesses and pus, but a more insidious low-grade indolent infection that only slowly develops, sometimes over months or even years. The bugs that cause this can be resistant to antibiotics and, once they have got hold in the biofilm around the implants, no amount of antibiotics will shift them. Finally the hip has to come out (sometimes there has to be a period of having no hip for a few weeks until the infection has gone) and then a new joint is implanted. This is all rather disappointing.

What are the chances of that? We cannot be completely certain but maybe 0.5-1% of replacements get infected within the first three month and at ten years, perhaps as many as 3-5% will have needed to be revised for infection.

Also, if you have a large metal and plastic/ceramic implant in your hip, infection elsewhere in the body can get in there and settle on the foreign material. Tooth abscesses, urinary infections and skin infections can all do it on rare occasions. Once you have had a new hip, it pays to get these things treated right away and not allow chronic sources of sepsis to go unchecked.

Thrombosis: Deep Vein Thrombosis (DVT) is a potential complication after hip replacement as it is for any big operation. Venous drainage from the leg is slowed up by the surgery and the time on the operating table and afterwards with no leg muscle contraction, are risks for this. Early mobilisation and avoidance of long periods of inactivity help reduce it and to supplement that, we ask patients to wear tight elastic stockings for 4-6 weeks to keep the superficial leg veins compressed, forcing blood to travel in the deep calf veins to prevent stasis and the chances for it to clot spontaneously. You will also get a blood thinner (Rivaroxaban), daily for 35 days. All these together make the risk no more than 1% and, nowadays, it is very rare to see a patient with a DVT.

Tip: WEAR THE STOCKINGS. They work.

Dislocation: Separation of the head from the socket is dreadful and extremely painful. It requires immediate hospitalisation and usually an operation to put it back in place. Once a hip has dislocated, it is more likely to do it again and the patient can lose all faith in it, feeling that they are sitting on a time-bomb.

Fortunately, it is very rare these days. A combination of increased femoral head size and improved surgical technique means that we see this complication after a primary hip replacement in fewer than 0.5% of cases. You will be shown how to safely move and walk and, within reason, unless you fall downstairs or are in a car accident, you do not need to worry about dislocation when doing 'normal' things.

You do NOT need to only lie on your back in bed for 6 weeks. Lying on either side is fine but, as I have found myself, this does not become comfortable for the first couple of weeks at least. (I am writing this at 0400 on day 12 as I keep waking up in pain rolling onto my side and I can't sleep on my back!) The hip is potentially more vulnerable to dislocation if you flex it beyond 90 degrees or cross the operated leg over the other one. Try and avoid these movements for at least 6 weeks. Once the new tough fibrous capsule has grown around the new hip by week 8-10, the risk goes away.

Leg length issues: It is pretty unusual for the hip to go in and make your leg too long or too short. There are ways of judging the correct length on the operating table and it isn't something we see very often at all.

But, if your leg has shortened during the run up to surgery, with some collapse of the joint and femoral head shape, you will have slowly adapted to a shorter leg, maybe without realising it. After the new hip has been implanted correctly, it may then feel too long for a few weeks until you adjust back to normal again. It is not uncommon for this to happen and my advice is don't worry; they usually sort themselves out.

Fact: Your pelvis and spine can accommodate for a 1-2 cm leg length discrepancy without you being aware of it and plenty of people have one leg longer than the other naturally.

Damage to nerves and blood vessels during the operation: This is very rare and modern surgery is much safer than it used to be in this respect. Never say never but this is not one to worry about.

Loosening: All implants will eventually fail *(if you live long enough)* and the commonest reason is loosening of the bond with the bone, whether cemented implant or press-fit. This usually starts slowly and insidiously with an ache in the thigh, then a pain, then more pain especially when walking. Patients sometimes say they have to 'bed in' the hip when they stand up before they can walk. Some have told me it is like having a loose tooth that you need to bite on before you can eat.

This should not be a near-term complication and over 80% of all implants will survive for 15 years or more. Early loosening is possible and then we mainly think it is due to low grade infection as described above. Excessive, especially high impact, exercise may predispose to this and it is seen more in the younger age groups. Some do, but I would not advise running, except perhaps for a bus, after a hip replacement. Why would you want to risk it?

These are the things I warn my patients about. One could go on but these are the big things with the big consequences. Fortunately, they are rare.

Again, hip replacement is safe. This means that the vast majority get through it without anything going wrong at all, and end up with a brilliant outcome.

NEVER LOSE SIGHT OF THAT.

MY HOSPITAL EXPERIENCE

Front door

Because of Covid, no-one can come into the hospital with you so after being dropped off outside in the rain at 0700 (early of course - army issue patient), someone has to be found to let you in. Also, due to Covid, the first requirement is to prove that your lateral flow tests have been negative, including the one that day at 0600. Hospitals have to make very sure that Covid doesn't sneak in with patients, so that's fair enough.

Even though I have worked there for 25 years, quite correctly I was processed as if I were a complete stranger, although there was no way I was having my bags carried for me or would be using the lift. Patients who don't have that ridiculous attitude are perfectly welcome to accept all assistance as offered of course. (At this stage I was still in the transformation phase from staff member to patient, which is my excuse).

Pre-op preparation

There's a lot to get through in hospital before you go to theatre. It seems like everyone is focused on you and helping you. They are the professionals and they have done it a thousand times, although the really good ones make you feel like you are their only patient, ever.

There's someone to take your details on arrival, there's someone to help you get ready for theatre, there's the ward stewardess wanting to know what you would like to eat when it's all over. The choices were sandwiches and also sandwiches. For variation I requested white bread but, as it is a hospital, such low nutrition fare was not an option. It did sound very likely that the crusts would be cut off though, so I didn't complain.

Then there's the anaesthetist who will be making your short stay with them pain free. In my case this was an old friend from the army and I knew exactly how it would be, having heard the mantra a thousand times. It's still a bit different when it's you in the hot seat.

The surgeon - never mind them, if they don't know what they're doing then you might as well stop reading now. With any luck you won't have to see or speak to them at all once you have signed the consent form. I actually helped train my surgeon - not a lot of patients can say that - I had started planning this day a long long time ago.

Off we go

At one time, until quite recently actually, you went down to theatre on your bed, wheeled by a porter and a nurse. The bed must go feet first as head first suggests that you are dead.

Why 'down' to theatre? My operating theatre was on the same level as the ward, but it's always 'down'. Maybe older hospitals always had the wards on the upper floors? Anyway, the trend now is for the patient to walk-the-walk, gown flapping open at the back, limping along in your slippers, and in my case through a phalanx of colleagues all wishing me well - like a celebrity, or maybe a prisoner. At a respectful distance behind comes the empty bed, as it is not yet on trend to walk back *after* the operation. Maybe one day patients will be asked to push the bed themselves?

In the anaesthetic room, having surrendered your spectacles and in my case, a false tooth, one lies down on the actual operating table so that no further transfer is needed once you are asleep. I had opted for a spinal anaesthetic (by far the best option if you can), which does involve some discomfort I must say. Although my anaesthetist is a magician, it is still a fairly robust needle and it does go in quite a long way. It doesn't take long and to be fair I have had dental local anaesthetic that felt worse. The effect is that your legs start to tingle and feel hot but before it's really working fully, the anaesthetist says good bye and...

...that's it. No dreams, no awareness, no banging of hammers or buzzing of saws. Nothing at all, seeming to last for about one second. When you wake up after a full night's sleep, you can tell that time has passed because you will have woken up several times during the night. Not so for this, it is total shut down of all awareness systems.

A blank screen, no cursor...

To recovery and beyond ...

Suddenly you are awake again after the operation and the nurse in recovery is making sure you really are OK despite all the carnage in theatre, and he or she is the one to welcome you back into the real world, a bit like a midwife for grown-ups. No bottom smacking though.

Sedative medication wears off very quickly (compared with a general anaesthetic), and I mean within minutes, but somehow she had managed to put my glasses on and get my front tooth denture back into my mouth before I was awake. Good skills!

Most people take some time to believe that the operation has actually been done and I must admit I did wonder if my surgeon had bailed out at the last minute, but eventually it dawns on you that this thing you'd been secretly dreading - especially if you know what really goes on - is actually over and that you survived!

Once they are happy you are stable and have stopped leaking blood and other stuff, it's back to the ward for post op care.

You are never alone

My recollection of that part is more or less continuous attention for several hours. You just doze off (because let's face it you have just had a tough two hours being asleep and all that), when your nurse is back to wake you up again to check your face works and that your blood pressure is still there. They need to make sure your temperature stays within the normal range and that all the main body systems are functioning. Just doing it once or twice won't do at all. At least every 30 mins is needed as things can go wrong occasionally and when they do, it can be quite fast. There are electronic aids for this monitoring; machines that go beep a lot and, hopefully, never go ALARM!!!.

If you have had a spinal anaesthetic (of course you have, it's the only way to fly), at some point you will start to regain feeling in your legs and other bits below the waist. This worked its way up from the end for me and the first part to come alive was my other leg, meaning one worked and one, well, just didn't. Odd that.

To wee or not to wee...

After an hour or two, you realise that you really do need a wee. I mean really. That feeling when you've had a few and you wake up in the middle of the night desperate for the loo... except you can't get up and stumble to the bathroom this time. Not only are you effectively tethered to the bed by leads and tubes, but there's the problem that your legs are not working properly and one has a 6 inch wound in it.

Hmm. You are not going to be able to sort this on your own for sure and this is where the nurse becomes your very special friend. Having announced that I needed to wee, like RIGHT NOW PLEASE, I was given the option of trying a bottle in the bed or perhaps sir would like to try sitting up and standing on his good leg?

Not being very supple, I opted for plan B as I thought it might stand a better chance of working, and should be less messy. Success! What a feeling. Never in the course of human experience is there a match for the overwhelming sense of achievement and satisfaction when you manage to wee post op for the first time. No one wants a catheter, and I certainly didn't seeing as I'd known the current staff in my hospital for at least ten years.

Apologies but I cannot really answer for the lady patients. (I did say this was about *my* experience). My nursing colleagues tell me that it is usually a bedpan, but a commode beside the bed can work for some patients, even on Day 1.

The trouble is once you start, there's no stopping and with in excess of 2 litres of fluid given during the operation, the next few hours gave me numerous opportunities to perfect my technique.

Up you get

Next, how about a little walk? I was lucky enough to have my operation early in the morning so by mid-afternoon I had been x-rayed, had lunch, Whatsapp'd everyone I know and accidentally sent an image of my hip x-ray to my entire family, rather than just my wife as I had intended. Oops. Gentlemen, please don't forget that more shows up on a pelvic x-ray than just the hips!

Tip: It may be best not to text or email anyone whilst the under the influence of strong medication.

So, the physiotherapist said, how about you put one leg in front of the other? And repeat. And repeat. Before I knew it we had gone the length of the ward and back. Again, I said. NO she said, that's it for today and she was so right.

Gradually increasing your walking is the key; it's a marathon not a sprint etc. And it has all got a lot of healing to do before there is anything approaching endurance again.

Nice to be up walking on day 1 though. Bit of a legend after that.

When can I go home please?

There is an increasing trend to try and do day-case hip replacement. It is perfectly possible to do this providing everything is planned carefully, the patient is robust and fit, the operation goes smoothly and the sun the moon and all the stars are spinning in perfect alignment.

I could have gone home on day 1, maybe not to Norfolk, but if I lived close to the hospital. My wife was a nurse so she would have been able to help me, and I would have been fine. I had a really straightforward operation, performed by a master surgeon, with a perfect spinal anaesthetic that wore off in two hours. As described in great detail, I was able to wee first time and I had almost no pain at rest and I didn't need illegal-strength opiate painkillers. I was able to walk within 6 hours of my operation and didn't faint. In short, I was extremely fortunate. *My* celestial bodies were all perfectly aligned (the x-ray confirmed that).

I was however, the exception, and years of this work means I know just how fortunate I was. Most patients don't get quite that lucky and although they thankfully usually do well, there's usually a B minus somewhere on their score-card. Striving towards day-case surgery is to be applauded. Let's just keep our common sense and not rush it or we, and some patients, will wish we hadn't.

Enough said, there was no way I wanted to go home that first day. It was much too much fun being in hospital and the food was excellent. I'll admit I was intrigued as to how it all worked down at bed level and to finally discover what my non-doctor colleagues' duties really entail. We consultants tend to waft into the patient's room, and say 'All well? Jolly good, carry on...' and that's it for the day. To see what really goes on and how the interactions, the observations and the pillow plumping actually happens is fascinating.

I also found out what can really irritate you. My biggest bug-bear was that there was no reachable plug socket for my phone and iPad. I could not believe it! Surely they knew that one's whole life revolves around one's phone? Texts, Whatsapps, emails, BBC news, even voice calls on occasion. And I am 60 – what if I were 25 and had never known life without my electronic life-partner? No matter how new your phone is, it still has to be charged. You use it so much lying in bed that it lasts less than a shift change and ... there was NO charger socket!!!

They have these on buses and trains nowadays, in bars and restaurants, in shopping malls, everywhere. But not in my hospital. The nearest wall socket was 2.4m from my bed. My lead is 1m in length. 'Please may I have an extension lead?' I ask. Against the rules in patient's rooms I am told. 'Please can we move my bed closer to the socket?' I ask, very slightly more firmly. Er, well as it's you, she says, and I am pretty sure that this might have been rather less possible had I not been the senior orthopaedic consultant in the establishment.

I have hope that, as a result of my gently worded suggestion in my satisfaction survey, phone charger sockets will soon be incorporated next to all the fancy bed positioning buttons on the bed frame.

But I would never have thought of that had I not been a patient.

Day 2

I would definitely have gone home on day 2 had I lived closer. I thought a 3 hour car journey would be a bit much though and my wife had a big day out planned. Having said that, I continued to learn a lot on that second day and had the opportunity to improve my moves under the strict eye of my physio colleagues.

Let me tell you about physios. They are extremely well trained practitioners and actually know far more anatomy and how the musculoskeletal system operates than we do. They are independent professionals and we forget that at our peril. Physio-terrorist is an endearing nickname, but I'd not advise using it within earshot of one.

Physios look nice, they smell nice, they speak nice ... but that's all a front. These people are HARD but they are FAIR. Because they are HARD, you will not like them. Because they are FAIR, you will LEARN. (With apologies to Gunnery Sergeant Hartman, Full Metal Jacket). It can't have been easy for these guys to work with me as a patient, but I made sure I played the part and so did they. I actually learnt stuff I should have known but didn't appreciate, like how to walk properly and how to do stairs safely.

Orthopaedic surgery without physio is like roast beef without horseradish: completely wrong and unfulfilling.

Anyway, that second day was good for practising my moves and planning a smooth exit from hospital.

Discharge planning

Discharge doesn't just happen, I realised. There are drugs to arrange, timings, anti-embolism stockings to pack, catering satisfaction forms to complete (easy that one – 5/5 for everything). In my case, a three hour journey was going to be required and hopefully that's not the case for you as it's a long time to be stuck in one seat, albeit with stops.

In the (good?) old days, you had to have had your bowels open before you could leave the hospital. I was quite prepared to lie if necessary but I am pleased to say that the current view is that it will happen when it's ready, which is so much more sensible. Everyone is different in this regard and insisting on performance prior to going home is silly.

It's a good idea to practise having a shower though. Modern wound dressings are made of industrial grade cling-film and can be relied upon not to leak, in either direction, so are safe to get wet on the outside. It's just a question of making sure you don't slip on the soap and is actually very achievable with minimal assistance, although I did realise that my nurse was poised to help if I had run into trouble.

The stockings: no-one likes these but they do help prevent deep vein thrombosis and believe me that is a complication you don't want. They are very tight to get on and it is not possible to do so on your own. I imagine if you don't change them at least every 48 hours, things will get very smelly and your toes will fall off. We all need *some* help.

A final thought. As I had my op in a private hospital I had a single room. This was nice for privacy but actually a bit lonely at times, especially as visiting was verboten due to that Covid tinker. I am no fan of the old Nightingale wards, but a 4 or 6-bed ward might have been quite fun to be honest, so if you're destined for that, don't be concerned. Almost all NHS elective orthopaedic wards are 'ring-fenced' now so everyone is in there for joint replacements and the like - plenty of kindred spirits to banter with.

So that was it, time to go. I pushed the wheelchair which was holding my suitcase, just because I could, and there was the car and my wife, waiting to take me home on country roads.

Hundreds of hip replacements are done every day in the UK and thousands worldwide. This was *my* journey and I have to say it was an enlightening and very very satisfactory episode. I am forever indebted to all the staff who cared for me and I can already say those amazing words that we love to hear:

It really has given me my life back.

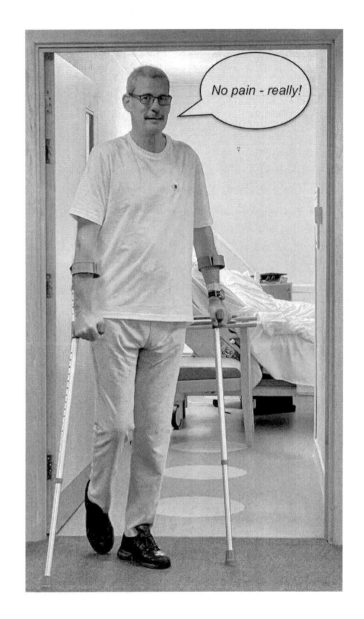

Day 2 post op

AFTERS

I will write this now (day 10 post op) and cover what I think is likely to be important over the next few weeks. I will then not touch it until week 6, and at that point I'll say how it really was.

So, you get home after all the excitement of the hospital experience and let's face it, it is quite an event and not something you will ever forget. But it just might feel a bit like the day after Boxing Day perhaps? It's still good but not quite the same. Your house turns out to be easier to navigate than hospital was and you realise that your stairs are achievable after all, so no need to sleep downstairs.

A tip on stairs - if you can acquire a third crutch, you can leave one at the bottom of the stairs when you go up and collect the third at the top. On the way down, it's the reverse. Saves trying to hold the redundant crutch while you are actually going up or down. Simple but effective, like orthopaedic surgeons.

DO NOT try to help. Let your other half/family look after you for the first week at least. They are primed for that and get very cross and worried if you seem to be doing too much. It's hard because so much of what we do at home is automatic and now you have to step back. Don't try and feed the dog, empty the dishwasher, do the washing up or even make a cup of coffee for yourself in the first week. I did all of those, or started to, and quite rightly got spanked for it.

After a week, well then it's open to negotiation. You have proven you are not going to fall over and your pain should have gone. It's still worth introducing these things gradually to avoid spooking the horses.

Exercises

THESE ARE VITAL FOR A GOOD OUTCOME. The exercises on the sheet provided in hospital are quite sufficient. But you have to do them properly and regularly. I would say three times per day is about right and 10-20 repetitions of each is sufficient.

Men, like small boys, tend to be unruly with this. They either do nothing at all, or more likely, go overboard. Anyone who has trained hard for sport just KNOWS that more is better when it comes to exercise and 'no pain, no gain' etc is engrained in the psyche. Eight times a day, 50 reps – good.

NOT GOOD!

A hip that is 20 years old and is surrounded by healthy young muscles can take it until you drop from dehydration and low blood sugar. You cannot do so much repetitive non weight-bearing exercise that you will hurt it.

A hip that has been, albeit beautifully and skilfully opened and closed, with clever repair of the muscles and other soft tissue CAN'T tolerate too much work. If you overdo it and go beyond the prescribed number of reps etc, things may start to fall apart. Suture lines take 6 weeks to be strong and I don't mean the skin here, but the muscles. Your surgeon has been good enough to put things back where they found them but please don't test the repair, it won't take it in the first few weeks.

Nothing appears untoward on the outside but the effect of those repair lines stretching and tearing at a microscopic level is that, when they do eventually heal, they heal long and with excess scarring. They still function but this may be at only 50% efficiency.

What does that mean for you? You might limp, or may do after a few hundred yards. You tire easily and never get back to the level of fitness you expected to. You have a dull ache in the hip. For ever. It's not bad but it always reminds you you have had a replacement. Nothing to be done about it, but it's a shame. *And* you blame the surgeon - not fair!

So, be good and don't go mad at first. Use the crutches properly and be careful. A fall is a disaster as you may well never get back to the right place, and if the hip dislocates? - just don't go there.

Walking

You were taught how to walk and do stairs. Do NOT feel the need to go home and not bother. The surest way to get a DVT is to sit around all day watching TV and eating in front of it.

If your house can accommodate it, make a circuit and do it once every hour or so. Do the stairs for exercise not just to go to bed. Go outside if the weather permits it. Try a short walk in the garden, or on the street if it's safe to. Once.

All this on the day after you get home. The next day, do a slightly longer walk outside. Only, say, 50 yards further though. Each day go further. Within a week, you will be doing the best part of a quarter of a mile.

Tip: Never go so far that you can't get back.

We are all different. But the principles of 'little and often' and small daily increases apply to everyone, whether you are 40 or 80. After a walk you may know about it and it will be 'achy'. If it's more than that, you are going too far or too fast. Listen to that. No pain... no problem.

Pain killers

These are good. Chances are you will have been discharged with more than you actually need. The rationale behind taking them regularly is that pain is easier to control if medication is taken regularly rather than on demand, and that sufficient pain relief is required to allow you to do the physio exercises properly (as above).

Fact: Most patients will not have any pain when sitting still or lying in bed after a week.

Fact: Pain when moving is a good indication that tissues are being stretched and a warning not to go too far.

So, where is the middle ground we are aiming for? You need some pain to stop you being an idiot and not so much pain that it stops you being a good patient by doing your exercises and keeping mobile.

We all feel pain in a different way. I feel qualified to know what is a 'good' pain and what isn't. But, am I really? I do know that within a day I had less pain at rest than I have had for the past 3 months. I do know that I found the first week pretty painful to sit down for more than 10 minutes without having to get up and walk about. You will have a different experience, and so will everyone else. It's personal, and we are not all the same. The pain that worries you may not worry me.

My advice: Take paracetamol every four hours, on the dot, all the time for a week. It will do you no harm and is not strong enough to let you be silly. For the first few days also take the stronger stuff (codeine, tramadol, oromorph etc) on the dot, every six hours. That should deal with the pain that might put you off doing your exercises. Then cut out the middle doses and take it every 12 hours for a few more days. Then after a week, try just the paracetamol and slowly cut out the middle doses of that over a few days. About day 10, try not taking anything and if you manage 24 hours without pain, you're there. At any stage, if you get rebound pain, go back to where you were and try again after three days.

That's the best I can offer. You will have to work it out for yourself but that's exactly what I have just done and I am now very comfortable, at rest and when exercising, after 24 hours 'clean'.

Swelling and bruising

This can be worrying. The thigh will almost inevitably be swollen for a couple of weeks post-op and sometimes this spreads down to the knee and beyond. There will always be some bleeding inside the muscles and this will often come out as bruising a few days after the operation. It may appear around the wound, in the groin or sometimes the back of the knee. I even had some around my ankle! The blood-thinner (Rivaroxaban) may make the skin bruise more easily as well.

But what if there's a DVT, you ask? As I said in the complications section, these are really rare nowadays but they can happen. The key thing is tight painful *calf* swelling which is tender to press and the skin might be hot and red.

If you get any of that, then you need to let the hospital know straightaway, and they will probably arrange for an ultra-sound scan to see what's what.

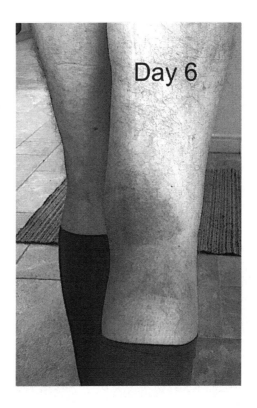

My right knee at 6 days. Impressive bruising!

Rest

You should be resting.

I got that a lot. So will you, and that's as it should be. A balance between lots of periods of rest and some sets of exercises and short walks is good. Your partner/family will always think you are doing too much at first and you may well disagree. As with all family disputes there is a good middle ground to be found.

Or, in the real world, just suck it up and do what the other half tells you.

Dedicated rest periods, especially in the afternoon are a good idea though. Go to your room and lie down. Read a book. Then wake up two hours later and wonder how you fell asleep.

Everyone feels worn out when they go home after this operation. The more blood loss you had, the more anaemic you are, the longer that goes on and it is completely normal to feel washed out for a month or so. DO NOT FIGHT IT. Go to bed early and get up late if you can. Be kind to yourself and let things heal and recuperate. Eat well, but not too much at once. Have faith. What about a drink? Nothing wrong with having one or two. If you have more than that and trip over your own feet and damage your hip, how's that going to feel?

Your body regards all this as a MAJOR injury and responds in exactly the same way as if you had been in an car crash and had broken your hip. All sorts of mechanisms are in play to correct for the damage and many are going on without you knowing it. Nature is good like that. Let it do its stuff.

Sex

I know, you're asking why has he included that? Both for completeness, as someone is bound to notice, and because it just might be why you bought the book. I'll keep it light.

Golden rule. Don't try it in the hospital. You laugh, but you'd be amazed at what goes on. Maybe not after hip replacement but...

It's a bit like the driving section:
Rule 1. Safety. People are genuinely worried about this and as I said earlier, you won't dislocate your hip doing 'normal things'. That said, no leg crossing or wide separation should be attempted before 6-8 weeks.

Rule 2. Comfort. One hopes traffic jams on the M25 don't come into play but you must be comfortable and relaxed. I suggest no sudden moves. You'll work it out.

Best estimate: 4-6 weeks. ('ish, again).

Week 6

Week 6, Day 42 at last. No mishaps have occurred and no wheels have fallen off. My memory of the hospital episode has faded but re-reading that section keeps it fresh. I sent a copy to the ward staff, and they seem to think it is a fair account on the whole. They also said it made them smile, so that's good.

So, how accurate were my predictions? On the whole pretty much I think. I did my exercises and added in new ones given to me during Zoom physio sessions with Fiona. I have worked alongside Fiona for the best part of 15 years but she still managed to treat me exactly like any other patient, without making any assumptions as to my level of knowledge. That's just as well as, as I said earlier, physios know far more about rehab than we ever will. She did not have to do her Gunny Hartman impression as I was meekly compliant and obeyed her instructions to the letter (army-issue patient).

As for pain, whilst at first there really wasn't any to speak of, probably because of the contrast with how my hip had felt before the operation, as I increased my exercise and walking, I began to get quite unpleasant groin pain. This came to my attention in a big way when I visited a garden centre on Day 30. Although I had been used to walking in straight lines for up to 7,000 steps per day by then, the stop-start-bend-twist-pivot actions that I was making while shopping were something new and had quite a marked effect. By the time I arrived home, I was pretty sore and it stayed that way for 48 hours. I knew what it was of course, and my chronically tight and inflamed hip flexor tendon – psoas – that crosses the front of the hip, arching around it, was definitely playing up and making its presence felt in a big way. A combination of lots of stretches, anti-inflammatories, and persisting with my daily walks got it to fade away but it wasn't much fun at the time. Longstanding hip disease often makes the psoas tendon tight and prone to inflammation, but it usually responds to the measures I have described.

I am much more upright than pre-op however, and have regained some of my 'military bearing', people tell me. I *do* feel a bit taller I must admit.

I did the driving 'test' last week and passed, and am happy to be back in my Land Rover again, confident and comfortable. Sleeping is just about there. For at least four weeks I struggled to be comfortable lying on my operated side. I could get to sleep but all too often woke up with an ache in my hip. That has almost gone and I have learned to sleep on my other side, something I could never do before the operation.

The wound has healed nicely but still itches - at times quite a lot, which is normal for a healing skin wound. Patients often tell me they use Bio-oil or Arnica cream or other such concoctions to improve the scar. I'm an ex-Para and I wouldn't want my scar to disappear altogether. It may not be a battle wound but it *is* a consequence of my army service and I shall regard it like a medal, for posterity.

Confession: As time went on I would sometimes walk into a room and then realise I had forgotten my sticks. Apparently that is quite normal.

Finally, have I achieved the ultimate aim of this operation, a 'forgotten' joint? It's very close and I know I will soon.

ADDENDUM

Things you worried about but didn't like to ask.

Will the spinal hurt?	A bit, but not as much as the dentist.
Will there be post-op pain?	Not as much as you'd expect and the drugs do work.
How will I poo?	More easily than you'd think. It's a good idea to practise beforehand by keeping your bad leg out straight and using your arms to lower yourself down. Try just putting weight on your good leg and if you can, do some press-ups or equivalent for a few weeks to improve your arm strength. Try to avoid getting bunged up and use laxatives if you need to.
How will I get dressed and undressed?	Ask for help; you'll need it at first. 'Grabbers' are useful for underwear.
What about shoes?	Wear slip ons. Also, because the stockings are slippy, if you pre-tie laces at the right tension, it's quite easy to get even lace-ups on with a long shoe-horn.
Can you actually feel the implants?	No. As far as your brain is concerned there is a gap where your old hip was, but it is too deep to be aware of. When you walk on it, all you can feel is sensation from the surrounding muscles and tendons.

Will I set off the alarms at the airport?	It's certainly possible. Wearing suitable clothing to be able to easily show off your scar is a good idea as they may want to see it, especially in the United States.
Will I feel like I have been given my life back?	You bet you will!
What should I give my surgeon? Anything else?	Your best efforts at the rehab and don't be stupid. Ask their secretary.

Post script

It is now 18 months since my hip replacement and I thought it may be of interest to tell the reader how things have been.

I can honestly say I have a 'forgotten joint'. I never really think about my right hip although if I find myself bending forwards and deeply flexing it, I do sometimes worry about going too far and risking dislocation. Although I know that this is most unlikely this far out because a tough capsule will have grown around the hip joint making dislocation almost impossible, I do still think about it.

Other than that, nothing. No pain, no squeaking, no feeling at all. In the first few months post op, I could get it to clunk a bit in certain positions, but now that the soft tissues have fully healed, this no longer happens.

My *other* hip, however, is a different story. Whereas at the time of my operation this was of negligible interest, it is now starting to feel like my right hip did in the year before I had it done. It's still manageable and I intend to wait until I fully retire next year before I have it replaced, but it's certainly getting there.

My new book, *'Waiting for a new hip? - tips to make your wait easier'*- is full of hopefully useful information to ease the symptoms of pain and stiffness as much as possible. My physio colleague, Fiona Goult has contributed with the exercise advice, and I have given the reader my opinion on how best to utilise pain medication.

If you are waiting for a new hip yourself, I really hope it helps.

Also available by Jonathan from Amazon.co.uk &
magicdaisy.co.uk:

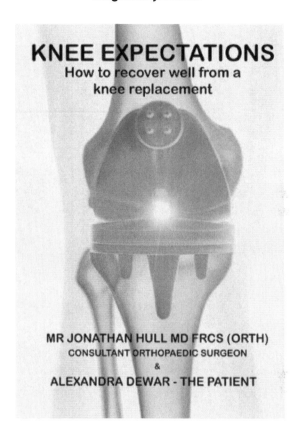

'...it doesn't put you off the operation, but with his humour, makes
you feel ready for the "ordeal"'- Martin (post-op patient)

Jonathan and Alexandra describe her experience and recovery
following her knee replacement. 5.0/5.0 rating on Amazon. £6.99

WAITING FOR A NEW HIP?

TIPS TO MAKE YOUR WAIT EASIER

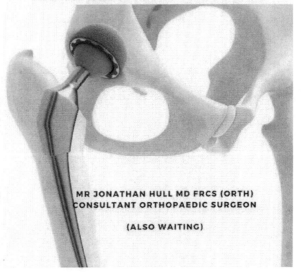

**MR JONATHAN HULL MD FRCS (ORTH)
CONSULTANT ORTHOPAEDIC SURGEON**

(ALSO WAITING)

While waiting for his other hip to be done, Jonathan has now written a comprehensive guide for patients who are stuck on the waiting list. Full of useful tips for dealing with a stiff painful hip, this includes very helpful information about exercise by Fiona Goult, physiotherapist, and medication advice.

'Easy to read and informative. Useful companion to have whilst waiting for a hip replacement'. Amazon review. £6.99

'Funny, sad and fascinating all in one book. Jonathan's style of writing is what I'd describe as easy, enjoyable reading' - Amazon review

This collection of bizarre but totally true case stories from Jonathan's 40 year career in both the Army and the NHS will amaze, amuse and shock you.

Not for the faint-hearted! Amazon. £8.99

ACKNOWLEDGEMENTS

My hospital stay was greatly enhanced by having a 'hip buddy' - my generous Foreword writer and consultant colleague Mr Henry Tilney. Henry was an outstanding man and it was a delight to spend two days of banter, laughs and non-stop chat, whether shouting across the corridor from our rooms which thoughtfully were directly opposite, or via Whatsapp which saved the other patients having to listen to our nonsense. Henry is a colo-rectal surgeon and knew no more about having a hip replacement than anyone else, so it was hopefully helpful having me to try and guide him along, just as I was finding out the real truth myself. We shared the highs (many) and lows (few), and there was a degree of competition about who could achieve what the fastest. Not a fair fight of course because I had the knowledge, and a 13 year age advantage, but we definitely both benefited from the experience and have remained close since, still competing to see who has walked the furthest each day and other meaningless milestones. He has helped me fashion this little book in lots of ways and his insights have been invaluable.

Huge thanks to my wife, Lorraine, not only for looking after me in her own inimitable and no-nonsense way, for keeping me from doing too much at the start and driving me everywhere (but not mad), and also for her advice about what I should, and more importantly, should *not* include in the text. And for her keen eye for detail, spotting my dreadful spelling and grammar.

As already said, I am totally indebted to all the staff at Spire Clare Park for taking such good care of me, especially Sharon who made it her business to nurse me more or less continually during my stay.

As for my surgeon, Richard Hargrove, he turned out to be every bit as good as I predicted he would be when he was my registrar in the early

2000's. He says he wasn't stressed by the prospect of operating on his former mentor, colleague and friend. Mrs H says otherwise! *(I am certain any one of my consultant colleagues at Clare Park would have done equally as good a job of my hip - RH just picked the short straw!)*

To Sam Pambakian MBE, outstanding anaesthetist, army buddy from as far back as the Eighties, Director of Critical Care for the 1st Armoured Division in Iraq during Gulf War 2, and Nightingale Hospital planner in the first Coronavirus wave - the spinal was excellent, thank you. *In Arduis Fidelis.*

I am most grateful to my many consultant, physiotherapy and nursing colleagues for their comments and suggestions to include things that I had missed, and also to Victoria Korzeniowska and Michelle Ford for giving me their views as recent THR patients.

The pen and ink cartoons were skilfully crafted by my son Richard, who is clearly wasted in hospitality. Those A levels in Fine Art and Graphic Design (double colouring-in) turned out useful after all.

Finally to my publisher, Magic Daisy, the creation of my clever daughter Charlie Bown (<u>not</u> Brown), who painstakingly edited the text, designed the covers and did the social media thing to help get it 'out there'- thanks Baby.

www.magicdaisypublishing.co.uk

Printed in Great Britain
by Amazon

37440167R00035